Copyright © 2020 All rights reserved.

Matt D'Aquino and Beyond Grappling retains 100% rights to this material and it may not be republished, redistributed or altered in any way without the written consent of Matt D'Aquino from www.beyondgrappling.com.
NOTICE: You do not have the right to reprint, sell, give away or share the content of this book
ALL RIGHTS RESERVED.
No part of this report may be reproduced or transmitted in any form whatsoever, electronic, or mechanical, including photocopying, recording, or by any informational storage or retrieval system without express written, dated and signed permission from the author. Thanks to Murray Simons, Xavier Barker and Craig Brown for your assistance putting this book together.

ISBN: 978-0-6489653-5-0

This book is dedicated to everyone who has had their life changed because of the work of Jigoro Kano.

Mamalithi ndrru'a lwamra mathamra, amra matha njenjenighinhikumu ngyunhu Jigoro Kano-ku.

The History Of JUDO
For Kids
By Matt D'Aquino
Illustrated by Craig Brown

Judo Cha Rrurimri
Lu Matt D'Aquino Ndudhuthu Ndrru'a Mamalithinjagha
Lu Craig Brown Mamalithingi Picha Njagha
Lu Xavier Barker ndudhuthu ndrru'a Mpakwithinjenighi

A Mpakwithi and English Bilingual Book

A long time ago in Japan, strong samurai warriors walked the streets. They were heroes in their towns and villages, and used jiu jitsu fighting techniques to challenge each other to see who the strongest fighter was.

Japanngi, amra Samurai (ma-twininga puthuku) tava mbrandrra laeghae. Amra ningi nje enam, jiujitsurru twiningafrighi.

During this time, a young man named Jigoro Kano was getting bullied at school. This was because he was smaller than everyone else. Someone told Kano that he should learn jiu jitsu techniques so he could defend himself.

Varaka, lu Jigoro Kano niighipwa schoolngu bullyghinhikamu. Lu pudhipwa, amra weeghe. 'ani ngyunhu chwagha: lu jujutsurru puthukunjengana.

Kano found a Sensei and began an intense training regime. Everyday he went to the training to learn how to fall safely, throw, trip, and sweep someone to the ground.

Lu Kano Sensei kanhangagha, lu punhukumu yughu tumana. Lu judo-training themechi angagha; lu ma njii'ghii, pughu.

He also worked hard to learn holds, escapes and joint locks while fighting on the ground.

Lu njanga judorru pughu. Lu ngyunhu ndrryamra dhayagha, lu njama maeghae.

He became highly skilled in only a few years, due to his dedication to learning and consistent training. After putting many techniques into practice, he discovered that a lot of them only worked if you were bigger and stronger than your opponent. This meant that someone of Kano's small size was at a disadvantage.

Lu judorru kati'i njenjenighi, themechi punhukumu. Lu techniqueithi pu-pughu; technique puchiki mapwaka yupatha. Lu Kano mapwa, kayunjenginhikumu.

He made it his mission to improve the techniques he was taught. Using his knowledge of how the human body moves and his love for studying other grappling arts, he began dissecting each technique in detail. He altered them in a way that allowed technique to overcome strength when applied with correct leverage and timing.

Lu Kano techniqueithi njenjengakunjaa. Lu Kano mathaka wa'athimri, lu techniqueiki wa'athimri. Lu Kano techniqueiki ndreeninjenighi, mapwa mbwiinhiikumu. Techniqueirri i leverageirri wambrama, ma-puthuku mbwiinii.

After years of study Kano put his new and improved techniques into an easy to follow system. In 1882, he opened his very own Judo school which he called the Kodokan. Kano's new grappling art was known as Kano Jiu Jitsu or Kodokan Judo.

Lu Kano sytemnga nje kayi-kayi technique chwakagha. 1882-ngu, ngyumra Judo-school pathagha – Kodokan ngyumra nduwidhi. Ngyumra Kano twininga-art njenjenga Kano Jujutsu ngyumra nduwidhi, Kodokan Judo ngyumra nduwidhi uwkunu.

Kano's system combined what he thought was the best parts of the jiu jitsu he studied. The three founding principles are:

- Maximum efficiency, minimum effort: using minimal energy or strength to defeat a bigger, stronger person.

- Mutual welfare, mutual benefit: living and training in a way that benefits everyone.

- Strive for perfection: Trying to be a better person by embracing honesty, kindness and teamwork in everyday life.

Lu Kano systemnga, lu Kano rungga-chwe-nje mbangagha. Rungga mbrandra chumu:

- Nhamra waka pudhipwa; nhamra result weeghe: mapwa ma puthuku mbwiinii, wakarra pudhipwa.

- Mbwi njenjenipri'i: kati'i ndrru njenjenini, mbwi njenjenini.

- Ndrru perfectionngi anga'a: ndrru yughu dhwimi'i, mbepenje, themechi nje pu'u.

Kano began teaching his martial art to everyone who wanted to learn— boys, girls, big people, little people, even old people. He developed it in such a way that you could practice really hard without getting hurt. To do this he removed or changed dangerous techniques and taught everyone how to fall safely. But most of all, he taught everyone to show respect to each other. He also emphasized the fact that Judo is more than just sport;
it is a way of life.

Lu Kano lwanha Judorru chaaghaa – niighithi, lanthithi, ma weeghe, mapwa, nduprighithi, wathayi, mawkiwghithi i lamalathithi. Lu Judo pathagha, mbwi chwe puthuku punu yughu dhayanhakumu.

Lu techniqueithi nggafra nyighi, lu mbunhu njii chaaghaa. Lu mbunhu chwagha - mbwi njenjenipri'i. Lu mbunhu chwagha: Judo ngge'e sport: Judo tavarra nje ndrrandathana.

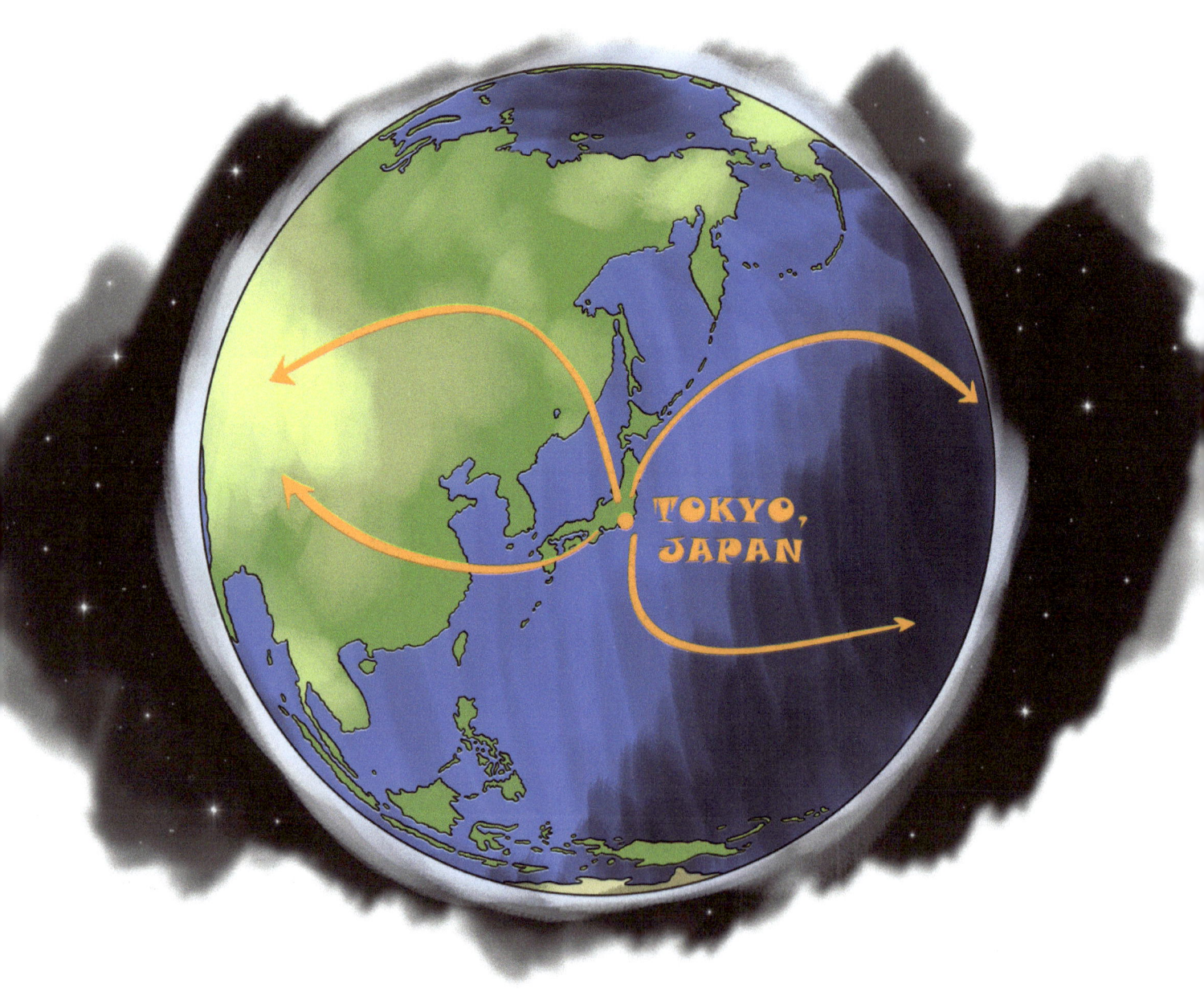

Over time Judo became very popular in Japan, and it was taken to other countries by Kano's students. Today, it is practiced in nearly every country in the world.

Matha puchiiki Judorru ntheyi pughu, Japanngi. Lu Kano studentthi Judorru ghunu wi, nggarru thaeghae. Judo nithingi kunu punu.

Judo training is a great place to have fun, make friends, develop self-confidence, self-discipline and learn effective self-defence techniques. There many ways you can be involved in Judo. You can do team and individual competition, kata, refereeing, coaching or simply train each week and have fun.

Mbwi Judongu pananjengana. Mbwi Judongu njenjengana, pay dhuwi-dhuwi-kuchana. Mbwi njenjenithini. Ndrru njumumu twiningana, yunjumumu twiningana, kata punu, refereeing punu, coaching punu. Ndrru Judorru themechi punu, njenjenithini!

We are so thankful for Kano's incredible ability to learn, study and develop such a great martial art. His perseverance and strength of character is something that many Judoka strive for.

Now you know the history of Judo up until today. What part will you play in its future?

Mbwi Kanoka njenjenini, lu wa'athimri, martial art chwe nje pathagha. Lu mbu'u puthuka, yughu thaeghae: mbwi Judoka puthukunjenganhakumu.

Ndrru Judoka kunu wa'athimrinjenini. Raerrae nhanha Judonga puyu?

About the Author:

Matt D'Aquino is a Judo Olympian and author from Canberra, Australia. He has represented Australia at eight Continental Championships, four World Championships and competed in the 2008 Beijing Olympic Games. He is also a Brazilian Jiu jitsu Black Belt.

Matt is passionate about teaching and has helped thousands of grapplers worldwide through his online Judo resources, eBooks and online content which can be found at beyondgrappling.com and universityofjudo.com.

About the Illustrator:

Craig Brown is a digital media professional and freelance artist based in the Northern Territory, Australia. Craig is a judoka with over ten years of experience in Judo, currently training and coaching at Top End Judo Academy. Craig loves Judo almost as much as he loves drawing, as Judo completely changed his life for the better.

About the Translator:

Xavier Barker is a revivalistics specialist with the Pama Language Centre, based in Cape York, Australia. Xavier also coaches No Limits (Special Needs) Judo and Kata at the Cairns Judo Club.

About Mpakwithi:

Traditionally, the Mpakwithi resided on country at the junction of Tent Pole Creek and the Wenlock River, on the West Coast of Australia's Cape York Peninsula. In 1963, their homes, school, co-op store and Church was razed to the ground by Queensland police to make way for a Comalco mining lease that still hasn't been realised. The population was split between towns at Napranum, Weipa and New Mapoon.

Today, sisters Agnes Mark, Victoria Kennedy and Susan Kennedy and their cousin Celia Fletcher work with Pama Language Centre linguist Xavier Barker to revitalize their language, recruiting new speakers all the time and developing novel and innovative ways to transmit the language.

More information on the Mpakwithi can be found at www.pamacentre.org.au/mbakwithi

www.ingramcontent.com/pod-product-compliance
Lightning Source LLC
Chambersburg PA
CBHW061135010526
44107CB00068B/2950